I0788682

This Book Belongs To:

____

BY
Home Planners And
Journals

This book is copyright protected. Reproducing this book is prohibited and not allowed without the permission of the author. All rights reserved.

www.ingramcontent.com/pod-product-compliance
Lightning Source LLC
Chambersburg PA
CBHW071221240726
48654CB00009B/876